Norn Irn
Joke Book

NORN IRN JOKE BOOK

© Copyright 2011

ISBN 978 0 95645 157 6
All rights reserved

Illustrations by Steven Brown

Published by

Causeway Press
9 Ebrington Terrace
Londonderry

jcprintltd
BELFAST
email: info@jcprint.net

Contents

Good News And Bad News

They had all passed away and President Obama from America and President Putin from Russia came up to the pearly gates along with the Rev. Ian Paisley. St. Peter informs them that the world is due to end in 24 hours and they must return and inform their respective Countries that the end is indeed about to come.

Obama goes on American television and says "Good people of the United States, I have good news and I have bad news, the good news is there is a heaven, the bad news is that the world will end tomorrow."

Putin then goes on Russian TV and he says "Comrades there is bad news and even worse news, most unfortunately for us atheists there is in fact a heaven, and the even worse news is that the world ends tomorrow."

Then it's Ian Paisley's turn on Ulster Television "Friends and dearly beloved of Ulster, I have good news and even better news" the population wait with bated breath as they have just heard the other two leaders on satellite TV and he finishes "The good news is that there is a Heaven, the better news is that there's never going to be a United Ireland"!!

"Gie her Lilty Big Lad"

Spectator urging a rather large base drummer in a band to continue playing loudly.

Telling The Future

Joan from Larne went to see a Psychic who was in town. Once in the darkened room the visiting Mystic Meg looked her straight in the eye, "I'm not going to try and kid you, there is some bad news here."

Joan "Oh dear what is it?"

Mystic "It's your husband."

Joan "What about him?"

Mystic "I won't lie to you, you and him have been married a long time, he is going to suffer from a very bad accident, and I'm afraid he won't be with you very long, you're going to be a widow"

Joan was very perturbed at this, took some time to compose herself then very slowly and softly said "What's my chances with the jury?"

"If them cats disnae quit their screekin I' m gonnae gie them what fer"
A man indicating to his wife that if the neighbours don't
get their cats to keep a little quieter at night
he will take drastic action.

Fix The Patient

A man isn't feeling well and goes to the Doctor, he takes his wife along for moral support. She sits in the reception as hubby is called in. Two minutes later the door opens and the Doctor comes out and asks the receptionist for a screwdriver, he then takes it back into his surgery.

Another minute passes and he comes back out again and asks for a pair of pliers, getting them he goes backing again.

Three minutes pass and out he comes once more this time he gets a claw hammer. The wife is really worried "Doctor, what on earth is the matter with my husband?"

Doctor "I'm not sure yet, but as soon as I get my medicine bag open I'll let him know."

Long Distance

The Boss was sitting behind the desk, not really concentrating on anything in particular when his secretary buzzed him on the internal phone; "Sorry to bother you Sir but it's long distance from New York."

The Boss who is still not concentrating replies; "It is that alright, about three thousand miles I think."

"Is that oul doll gonnae squak there al night?"
Man complaining to his friend in cinema about an elderly lady who insists on giving a running commentary on the film.

"It' ll nat be lang nai till she's away, the size o her"
One young woman to her friend describing another
female whom she has just met and who is obviously
about 8 months pregnant.

Surprise Prayer

The new Minister had begun his visitation and arrived at a very isolated family home and as it was late in the evening and in winter the family insisted that he must stay overnight.

The Father says "Your Reverence we'll gladly put you up for the night, unfortunately we're not that well off out here in the sticks so hopefully you don't mind sharing the room with our young son Billy here."

"Not at all, that will be fine" replies the Minister.

He then goes into the small bedroom and notices that Billy is kneeling by his side of the bed. "This is very good and should be encouraged" he thinks and tiptoes round the bed to kneel beside the young boy.

"And what are you doing Reverend?" says Billy.

"Well Billy, I'm just doing the same as you" he smiles.

Billy replies "Oh boys but you're in trouble wi me mammy then, for there's only one potty, and I'm using it."

Fast Prayer

A young Presbyterian Minister had been trying to get a 'call' to a church, he had preached in a number of Churches and wasn't having any success.

As time wore on and he still had no success he was getting a bit desperate, then one morning a letter arrived. He opened it, smiling he showed the contents to his wife who said; "I think we should pray about this dear."

Young Minister replies "You pray, I'll pack."

Chinese Patient

A very diligent man likes to call with sick friends to see if there is any help or comfort he can offer them.

One day he goes to his local hospital to see a very ill friend. As he is finishing with his visit he notices an elderly Chinese man in the bed opposite who has had no-one visit him in the time he has been with his friend. He goes over to the Chinese man and speaking slowly he says; "I – HOPE – YOU – WILL – SOON – BE – BETTER"

The Chinese man replies "Ah kamie ah so da loh"
Visitor "I – AM – SO – SORRY – I – DON'T – SPEAK – ANY – CHINESE"

The answer comes back ""Ah kamie ah so da loh"
He sees that he's really not going to make any progress so he smiles very sweetly and says "WELL – I'LL JUST – GO – ON – NOW –AND – EVEN – THOUGH – YOU DON'T – UNDERSTAND – ME – I – HOPE – YOU – WILL – SOON – BE – BETTER"

As he's leaving the ward the beeper beside the Chinese man's bed goes off, the cardiac team rush in and they try and resuscitate him but to no avail. He passes away.

The visitor goes home and tells his wife who is horrified. Then on the Friday his wife is going to their local Chinese restaurant for a carry out. Hubby says "When you're down there ask them what "Ah kamie ah so da loh" means as those were the old man's last words to me. It must have been very profound cause he said it twice.

The wife comes back with the carry out, glaring at hubby; "Ah kamie ah so da loh, is that what he said?" she says, not looking pleased at all.

"Yes why?" says the husband, "What does it mean?" Wife "It means, You're standing on my oxygen cable!!!"

Guilty Charge

A man is up in Court on a charge of theft of a TV. He's not really that smart but he knows enough to get an expert solicitor who puts up a very good defence and the verdict is given by the Judge of not guilty.

Looking down over his glasses the Judge, who is not entirely convinced says "I am finding you not guilty as on the balance of probabilities there is not enough evidence to convict, but you must not appear before me ever again, do you understand?"

"Yes M'lord, does this mean I can keep the TV?"

"He's poundin that dure lik he wud wake the dead"
A neighbour complaining that the next door visitor
is knocking very hard at the front door.

Saw Nathin

Johnny got himself killed in a car crash, so he arrived at the pearly gates.

Peter is standing with a clipboard, he says "Jehovah's Witness?"

Johnny replies "Well, to be quite honest, it all happened that quick I didn't even see the accident".

"Thon's niver affside, ya buckeejit ye"
A football spectator complaining that the referee did not interpret the offside law correctly.

Not The Normal Car Wash

The man at the car wash in Aberdeen says "That will be £3.50 please sir, we don't get that many Irishmen in here."

Paddy says "How did you know I was Irish?
Man says "Well, there's not too many boys come in here on a motorbike!"

Too Much Tax

Two Irishmen are walking along Oxford Street in London, Seamus looks down at his feet, "Boys o boys, look what I've got."

Paddy says "What is it Seamy?"

Seamus says, "Dae ye not see, it's a pay packet."

Paddy looks at it and says "Ach that's ridiculous so it is."

Seamus looks at him flabbergasted "Whaddya mean ridiculous?"

Paddy replies "Shur look at the much tax they tuk aff ye."

"Sardy wan the day nai"
A greeting indicating that it is a bit cold today.

Good Weekend For Some

On Monday morning at work Davy shouts over the factory floor "Hi Jimmy, what were you at over the weekend?"

Jimmy "It was great, spent all day Saturday shooting duck."

Davy "Sat-rite, were they wild?"

Jimmy "Well they let's just say they weren't best pleased!"

"The mower's stickin out, ye cudn't bate it"
The owner of a new lawn mower telling
a friend how good it is.

Wrong T-Shirts

A Belfast woman brings her misbehaving boy along into a T shirt shop in Portrush; "See them T-shirts ye's hav outside, the wans way the latters on them, I want wan fer the boy here" she says pointing at the son.

"Yes Ma'am" says the assistant "Which letter would you like on the T shirt?"

"Oh it has tae be Q" she says.

The assistant disappears into the back of the shop, comes back five minutes later and tells her there are no shirts with the letter Q.

"I'm really sorry, it's just we never get anyone whose name starts with Q."

The Mother drags the boy out of the shop lecturing "Didn't I tell ye they wudn't have anything fer ye Qhughie."

Long Journey

The Ulsterman was in London and he got into the Black Taxi.

Driver "Where to Sir?"

Sammy "Waterloo."

Driver "Is that the Station?"

Sammy "Well, I'm a bit late for the battle."

Sound The Alarm

Young Rickie is misbehaving quite badly at home so his Mother tells him he has been bad all week and is being sent to bed early.

After an hour he shouts down "Mum, can I have a glass of water?"

Mother says "Indeed you cannot, that's just an excuse to get back down again, anyway you had a glass before, you can't be thirsty again."

Rickie says "I know, but the bedroom's on fire."

"Them new purties are a dasparate price agin the year"
I see the new potatoes have gone up in price again this year.

Wrong Answer

The recession is hitting hard so three men, a Scotsman, an Englishman and an Irishman apply for security jobs on a building site. They know each other quite well so they agree that if they can help one another at interview they will.

They go into the foreman's hut and he tells them he has some basic questions to ask each of them. "There's some racketeering going on here so I just want to make sure you know about that."

First question to the Englishman "What do the letters INLA stand for?" The Englishman thinks for a moment and the Irishman whispers to him "Irish National Liberation Army."

"Very good" says the foreman suitably impressed.

Now to the Scotsman "What do the letters UVF stand for?" The Scotsman hesitates then Paddy whispers again "Ulster Volunteer Force."

NORN IRN JOKE BOOK

"Good stuff" the foreman says.

Finally it's Paddy's turn "What do the letters DIY stand for?"

Paddy's completely lost at this but his two mates whisper to him "Do It Yourself."

Paddy jumps up and says "This isn't on, I helped you two get the right answers."

A Very Helpful Wife

A man and his wife are out together on a Saturday night, on the way home they are stopped by a Police checkpoint.

"Good evening Sir, I notice you haven't got your seatbelt on tonight" says the constable.
"Yes constable, I am very sorry about that I always do wear it, I just forgot" says the Husband.

Leaning over the wife says "Constable, I'm forever mindin him about that seatbelt, he always forgets it."

The husband smiles nervously at the police officer. "Do you also realise you were 10 miles per hour over the speed limit Sir."

"Oh dear, officer, that is really unusual, I normally drive very slowly and carefully."

Again the wife intervenes "He's aye drivin too fast if you ask me."

The Constable then says "Do you and your wife not get on too well sir."

Before the dejected husband can even start the wife says "He's only as bad as this when he's had a few drinks."

Starting Up In Business

An Irishman is starting up in business in Birmingham, he is handing out his newly printed business cards on the High Street. After a short while a man who has taken a card comes back over to him and says; "Excuse me squire but why are your cards blank?"

The Irishman smiles and says "Well, to be sure, your always better being careful when ye start out so I want to remain anonymous."

Cut Price Robbery

The Police were called out to a shop which had been burgled.

The Policeman says to the shop owner "This looks pretty bad, did you lose much?"

The Shop Owner says "Oh it's bad alright, they stole loads of stuff, but I'm just glad they didn't come last week."

"Why's that then?" says the Officer.

Shop Owner says "Well we just started a big sale on Monday."

"If the cub's half the man his oul boy is, he'll be a good'n"
An observer of a family pointing out that if the young son turns out to be even half as good as his father he will do quite well for himself.

❖ ❖ ❖

"I wis feart he wud ate the leg aff me"
A postman indicating to the householder his fear
of the lively looking dog in the garden.

A True Friend

A young woman was not long married but things had started to go wrong. She decides to phone one of her old friends from school for help.

Wife "Hello."

Friend "Hi."

Wife "Ah'm havin wile trouble wi the man, ah'm doin all I can but it's nivver right."

Friend "Oh that's terrible."

Wife "It's dasparate, if it's not the breakfast, it's his dinner, everythin's wrong."

Friend "Oh my, that is bad."

Wife "Ach it's even worse than that, the shirts aren't ironed right, he says he does his fair share an I mess things up."

Friend "Oh, this sounds serious."

Wife "It is, It is, wud ye do me a favour."

Friend "What kind of favour."

Wife "Wud ye come over and jis gie me a wee hand out, nothin big, just tae get me back intae the swing o things."

Friend "Sorry but who is this again?"

Wife in indignant tone "Its me, Rachel yer friend from Archdale Secondary."

Friend "I never attended Archdale Secondary"

Wife "Is that Belfast 51276"

Friend "No. this is Belfast 51277"

Wife pauses for a few seconds;

"Does that mean, yer nat comin over then?"

"Ye're takin a han o me aren't ye?"
When told a story that seems most unusual this is a
typical Ulster person's response.

Asleep Or What?

The District Council had been very annoyed at the way the local newspaper had been covering Council meetings. When the paper said in a front page story that at a recent Council meeting half the members were asleep, the Mayor was furious.

He got in touch with the Editor and demanded an apology, then he went before the Council to inform them that he had taken the appropriate course of action. The following week the Paper ran the headline "We apologise for last week's headline, half the Council were not asleep!"

Nathin Till Bate The Ulsterman

A Polish man had arrived to work as a supervisor in Northern Ireland. He was trying to cope with the English language but it was nothing compared to the Ulster version he encountered on the shop floor. He had to deal with a dispute between two men.

"You are saying the other man is not being reasonable" said the supervisor.

"Aye" replied the Ulsterman.

"In what way?" the supervisor inquired.

"He's aye eatin the face aff me" said the workman.

"I'm very sorry, but what do you mean?" said the supervisor getting worried.

"Look, he niver talks till ye but he's jumpin down yer throat" said the workman really getting worked up.

"But I don't think anyone could do that" said a wide eyed supervisor.

"Well he can, shur he's niver done chewin the rag" replied the worker.

At this point the visiting supervisor just rolled his eyes and gave up.

Big Rhubarb

The newly weds were getting used to married life, the hubby said to his wife as he left for work, "I would really love rhubarb tart for sweet tonight dear" he said. She finished her own work that day and set about baking the tart, but she hadn't done this before. Evening came and she set down the finished rhubarb tart on the table. "Let's eat" says she. "What sort of an appetite do you think I have?" he says, "that tart must be nearly two feet long".

The wife says "I know that, but I searched everywhere and they were the shortest stalks I could get."

Twelfth Holidays

An Ulsterman is keen to book his holiday in Brighton during July, so he writes to a Guesthouse asking can he make a booking for the twelfth week in July. The Landlady wrote back apologising as in England July has only four weeks.

"Them weans wud deeve yer head al day"
A typical Ulster response to children being quite boisterous during the school holidays.

Leaving For The Better

A Minister is leaving his small rural parish and as he makes his final visits he tells one elderly lady "Don't worry now that I am going, because you'll probably get a better Minister than me the next time."

The Lady replied "I'm not so sure, the man we had before you said the same thing."

"Jurin the troubles we gat our windaes and dures put in regular lik"
An Ulster family telling a visiting journalist that during the troubles their home was under attack on a regular basis.

Pricy Nowadays

A young boy was in Sunday School and the teacher was stressing the need to say grace before meals, "It's really important to thank God before you eat your food" she says. "Johnny, what does your dad say before you begin your family meal?"

Johnny "Please Miss, he usually says, Go easy on the butter, for it's got wile dear these days."

How Many Sheep?

A Bishop from the City went on holiday to a little guesthouse in Wales so he could get away from the clamour of the City. He wasn't dressed in his clerical clothing as he went out for a walk one day and met a local man, after the usual general chat about the weather he asked the man; "And what do you do for a living?"

"I'm a farmer" said the local.

"And what do you farm?" inquired the Bishop.

"Oh, I have the sheep now" he says.

"And would you have many sheep" asks the Bishop.

"I do, I have 143 to be exact" he says and just to turn the tables a bit he asks the Bishop "And what would you do then?"

The Bishop replies "Well I suppose I'm a shepherd like yourself."

At this point the farmer looks at the Bishop's fine jacket and his smooth hands with some disbelief; "Is that right, and how many sheep would you have then?"

Thinking in the spiritual realm the Bishop replies "Oh I can't be as precise as you but about ten thousand."

The farmer is really exasperated at this, "Ten thousand, t-e-n thousand he spells out, boys you'd have a divil o a time at the lambin then."

Through Thick And Thin

Sharon's husband had been very unwell for several months. He had been married before and was quite wealthy. Things looked pretty bad for him, but she was by his bedside every day. One day he was keen to talk, he motioned for her to come closer. She pulled the chair up to the bed and leaned her ear close so she could hear him.

"You know" he whispered, his eyes filling with tears, "You've been with me through all the bad times. When I lost my job, you stuck right beside me. When that business I started up went under, you were there. When we lost the house, you were there. When I was in that car accident, you stuck by me. And now that my health has got bad, you're still by my side. And you know what?"

"What, dear?" she asked gently, smiling to herself.

"I think you're bad luck."

Time For Dinner

A couple with a family had invited their elderly
Minister who was nearing retirement, round for
Dinner. The Minister arrived a bit early and he was
taken into the front sitting room where young Samuel
was playing. The couple told the Minister the meal
would be ready shortly and young Samuel would keep
him company while it was being served.

The Minister asked the little boy "Well Samuel, what
are we having for Dinner tonight?"

Young Samuel "We're havin Goat."

Minister "Oh Dear, Goat!, are you really sure that's
what we're having for our meal tonight?"

Young Samuel "Definitely, I heard me Daddy sayin to
me Mammy this mornin, the day's as good a day as
any tae have the oul goat for Dinner!"

"Thon boy's the size o tuppence and the rattle o ninepence"
That rather small chap seems to talk quite a lot to
make up for his size.

50

Memory Not The Best

Three elderly Belfast men go to their Doctors. They're all concerned at their failing memory. The Doctor knows that they were never the brightest so he puts each of them to a simple test.

To the first he says, "What is three times three?" "134" came the reply. The doctor rolls his eyes and looks up at the ceiling, and says to the second man, "Ok now your turn. What is three times three?" "Wednesday," says the second man. The doctor shakes his head sadly, then asks the third man, "Okay, your turn. What's three times three?" "Nine," says the third man. "That's great!" says the doctor. "How did you get that?" "Simple," he says, "just take 134 from Wednesday."

"Tak yersel away aff and dinnae be borering me agin"
A lady telling a man not to be bothering her again
as she does not like him.

The Man For The Job

A young Omagh man had successfully applied for a job in a large store. The Manager had seen quite a few like him before so he greeted him warmly and took him down to the shop front and said, "Now your first job will be to sweep the floor completely clean in the morning" pointing at the broom leaning against the wall.

The young man looked horrified and said "Perhaps you didn't look at my CV but I graduated at Queens University in the summer."

"Oh I'm sorry, I didn't realise that, here give me the broom I'll show you how."

Great Antlers

An Ulster couple were on holiday in Glasgow and were having a look round an antique shop. The lady noticed a rather grand set of antlers and asked the shop owner how much they were, "£75" she was told.

"They're affa dear" says the wife. The owner replied, "Aye they are, did you think they were aff a greyhound?"

"She's rite n lite on the juice now sir"
The second hand car salesman explaining that the vehicle he is trying to sell has got quite a high miles per gallon ratio.

"Ye' ll hae tae dance on yer pins tae avoid the cow clap in here"
A farmer telling a city person to be very careful how they
walk in the field due to the number of cows grazing
and the deposits left by the cattle.

American Politics

A very aggressive senator in the USA was known to be a bit of a bully. His speech writer was good and was asked to do all his speeches, short, medium sized and very long ones, he wrote them all.

After a year the senator got so full of himself and he had gotten to know the speechwriters style he hardly bothered looking beyond the first page of a speech that was written for him. The writer knew he was good so he goes into the senator's office and asks for a pay rise. The senator is in a foul mood and is so full of himself he says "You don't deserve any pay rise, in fact I don't need you anymore, clear your desk and get out, now."

The speechwriter is dumbfounded, goes back into the office, clears his desk and goes. That afternoon the senator is booked to speak at a press conference. The assembled scribes, radio hacks and TV presenters are

all present.

The senator stands before them all "Ladies and Gentlemen, I stand before you today" he glances down the prepared script, smiling to himself thinking this is too easy, "prepared to do whatever I can to help the automobile plant here in this City," he's approaching the bottom of the page "I now wish to unveil a fifteen point plan to help save the five thousand jobs here" the cameras are running, the hacks are straining on every word, he turns to the next page and there in large hand written letters are the words in large type; "On your own, sucker!"

Chainsaw Expert

An Irishman called Dermot moved to Canada looking for work. After some time Dermot called at a timber company, the foreman says "Right Dermot, start work tomorrow and we'll see how you go for a week or two, but we expect every man to work hard here, no slackers" and he points over to the stack of trees lying after being felled.

"No problem sir, I'm a hard grafter."

The next day he turns up and his superior points to the chainsaw, "The next batch of trees are down the hill, we'll see how you get on tonight."

He arrives back in the evening with sweat on his brow and his shirt, the foreman says "Well, how'd the day go?"

"Aye not bad" he says

"But how many trees did you fell?" says the boss

"Three" says Dermot

"Three!!" replies the boss "We expect ten per day per man, well let's see how it goes tomorrow."

The next day Dermot is up early and goes at the trees really hard, back at the foreman's hut in the evening with even more sweat the boss asks, "Well how many today?"

"Four" he says.

The Boss says "Right, I know you're only two days at this, but looking at the state of you, at this rate you're never going to get up to ten a day, what's the problem?"

Dermot says "Well that chainsaw's not too sharp."

Foreman "That's a brand new saw, here let me see it" and with that he reaches for the chainsaw, quickly examines it, pulls the ripcord and as the saw roars into life Dermot shouts "Hey, what's that noise?"

Milk, Milk, Milk

The young boy got into trouble at home and was ordered up to bed early. He got in bed and then asked his dad for a glass of milk, so his dad brought him up a glass.

Five minutes later the boy called down to his dad, "Can I have another glass of milk dad?"

So, his dad brought him up one. Five minutes later the boy called back down, saying "I want just one more glass of milk dad."

His dad said "NO, if you ask me one more time I'm going to come up there and spank you."

There's silence for a minute then the boy called down, "Dad, on your way up to spank me can you bring me a glass of milk?"

"The nites are away wi it shur an its ony august"
This is a regular Ulster expression heard during the month of August to indicate that the evenings are already getting darker.

Absolutely Dead Sure

Two men from Bangor, Davy and Jimmy, were out shooting pheasant. They get to the site and start walking.

After about a half hour of walking, they sit down and take a rest.

Davy says to Jimmy "I'm not feeling very well."

Jimmy says "We'll go back to the cars."

Davy says "OK, lets do that."

So they start going back. About 10 minutes later, Davy falls over, out for the count, Jimmy panics and calls 999.

The operator answers "999, which emergency service?"

Jimmy says "My friend fell over with a heart attack, I think he's dead, what should I do?"

Operator says, "Well, first make sure he's dead."

Jimmy says, "Ok."

The operator listens and hears a very loud BANG!!!

Jimmy gets back on the phone and says, "Ok. He's dead … what now?"

Sleeping Problem?

Willie had this problem of getting up late in the morning as he couldn't get to sleep until the early hours and was always late for work.

His boss was fed up with him and threatened to fire him if he didn't do something about it. So Willie went to his doctor who gave him a pill and told him to go to bed early and take it as it would give him a good night's sleep. Willie slept well, and in fact, was up before the alarm in the morning. He had a leisurely breakfast and drove cheerfully into work.

"Boss," he said, "The Doctor gave me a pill and it worked great!"

"That's all fine," said the boss, "But where were you yesterday?"

"I gien that targe doon the street a piece o my mind the day so I did"
Wife telling husband that she has spoken very strongly
to a lady in the street who has a bad reputation.

Supplies

The foreman of a building site in Antrim had just been sent 3 new recruits. Two of them were big strapping men while the third was a small Japanese man.

"OK" The foreman says pointing to the two big men, "You two get up to the roof and hoist up the materials, and you, pointing to the Japanese "your in charge of supplies, over there" pointing to the stores.

After about two hours the two men come into the site hut complaining, "We can't get any work done."

Foreman "Why not?"

Men "The Japanese isn't getting us any tools."

The Foreman goes straight out to the store and seeing no one about he shouts "Where are you?"

The Japanese jumps out from behind the counter and shouts "Supplies, Supplies."

Half Man Half Animal

The teacher wanted to introduce ancient Greek mythology very gently into the classroom so she asks; "Who can tell me the name of the person in greek mythology who was half man and half animal?"

Quick as a flash wee Jonny puts his hand up "Please Miss!"

The teacher is impressed and says "Well Jonny you're very quick off the mark today, who is it then?"

Jonny "Easy Peasy Miss it's Buffalo Bill"

Father And Son

Son says to his Father "Dad, I have a very hard algebra homework which I have to do for the morning, will you do it for me?"

Dad "No son, you need to learn these sorts of things yourself, it just wouldn't be right."

Son "Well at least you could try."

"When yer comin, jes come roun the back fer fear I' m nat in"
This would be a telephone conversation between the woman of the house and a person who will be calling, and the visitor is told to use the rear door which is left open in case the house owner has just gone out.

Height And Weight

A rather overweight man from Lurgan is sent to the Doctor by his wife.

"You be sure and get somethin aff the Dactor, yer putting on the pounds something fierce" she says a little too directly.

"Aye, alrite" he says putting on his jacket as he goes out the door.

An hour later he arrives back with a mischievous smile.

Wife "Whit are ye grinning at, whit did the Dactor say?"

Husband "He measured me up and got me to stand on wan o them scales that gives yer height and what weight ye shud be."

Wife "And whit? Shur you musta been miles out."

Husband "Naw, I'm the right weight, ah just have tae grow another 10 inches."

Speaker's Ruling

A Member of Parliament rises to his feet, "Mr. Speaker, this is downright disgraceful, the Honourable Member opposite who has just spoken has brought the House into disrepute."

Speaker "How did he do that?"

M.P. "For the ten minutes before he got up to speak he has been acting the fool."

Speaker " Order Order, I regret to inform the Member who has raised this that the MP he refers to was not acting!"

"The oul boy' ll be in wile late an him haf lit"
This is a younger family member telling a friend that the father of the house will be quite late coming home and when he does he may well be in a drunken state.

Mum As Well

Mr. Armstrong sat down with his daughter and smiling very sweetly told her, "Your young man told me tonight he wanted you for his bride, and I gave my consent."

"Oh, Daddy," gushed the daughter, "That's brilliant it's going to be so hard leaving Mummy."

"Well I understand that," beamed Daddy. "Sure you just take her with you."

"I canny gleek out the drapes, but he's aye gien me a lecture"
The somewhat curious wife who is frequently peering out of the window to see what is going on, much to her husband's annoyance.

Not Known In Church

An elderly lady arrives for the service in a country Church, an eager young Committee member helps her up the steps, "Can I show you to a seat, where would you like to sit?" he says.

The elderly woman says "Thank you so much young man, I would like to sit right at the front so I can hear everything that is said."

The young man leans in close and says "You wouldn't really want to sit at the very front as the Minister here can be very boring."

She replies "Young man do you know who I am?"

Young man "No I'm sorry, I don't know you."

Elderly woman "I'm the Minister's mother."

Taking a very deep breath he says "Do you know who I am?"

She replies "No, I do not."

He says "Good!"

Hen Problem

Sammy goes to the Doctor, "Doctor, my wife thinks she's a hen."

Doctor "That's just ridiculous, how long has she suffered from this condition?"

Sammy "About three years."

Doctor "Three years! Why didn't you do something about it sooner?"

Sammy "Well, we needed the eggs!"

Conversation

A middle aged woman who was a bit of a 'plain jane' was on the train from Belfast to Ballymena. At Antrim Station a foul mouthed dishevelled man who was obviously quite drunk got on board and sat down opposite her. After some attempted conversations by the drunk the woman says, "You are the most disgusting man I've ever met and you are very VERY drunk."

The drunk looks at her and says, "Shur yer nat much better lookin, but at least I'll be sober in the morning."

"If yer goin on ahead out lik that ye'll be foundered"
Father indicating to his daughter that if she goes out without a coat in the wintry weather she will feel the cold a lot.

Chicken Theft

The Catholic Priest was in the confessional box in Carrickmore when a young man came in; "Bless me Father for I have sinned" he says.

Priest "What have you done my son?"

Man "I stole a chicken Father, would you take it?"

Priest "Of course not, you need to give it back to whoever you stole it from."

Man "I offered it to him and he wouldn't take it, Father."

Priest "Oh well then you might as well keep it, four Hail Mary's and don't do it again."

The Priest leaves after confession and returning to his home discovers that one of his chickens is missing!

"Ma stummick thinks me throat's cut"
A man indicating he is very much in need of a drink
and hasn't had one for quite some time.

No More Eggs

A driver out in the countryside stops at a farmhouse where there is a sign which says 'FARM EGGS ON SALE HERE'. He knocks on the door and the farmer's wife appears.

Driver "I see two of your hens have stopped laying"
Farmers wife "Well how on earth would you know that?"

Driver "Because I've just run over them."

"He wudnae be the sharpest pencil in the box"
A description of a person who wasn't regarded as being very bright.

Pray Out Loud

The young boy had been taught to always pray before going to bed. One night in December he's upstairs and he starts "God Bless Mum, God Bless Dad, God Bless my brothers and sisters and especially bless my lovely Grandma."

His Mum and Dad downstairs hear the prayers through the open door and smile at the lovely thought. Then the prayers get louder "Dear God please don't forget about my motor scooter for Christmas."

Mum goes up and says "Jonathan, pray quietly, there's no need to shout you know. God's not deaf."

Jonathan replies "I know that, but my Granny is."

Teaching Profession

A very stressed out teacher is at a seminar and the Lecturer starts off "Right, I want someone to give me two short and succinct reasons for entering the teaching profession, no elaborate answers now."

Teacher "Simple enough, July and August!"

"He's been racin pigeons for donkeys"
A man in the locality has the pastime of breeding racing pigeons for many years.